KS2
7–8
Years

Master Maths at Home

Addition and Subtraction

Scan the QR code to help your child's learning at home.

DK | **MATHS NO PROBLEM!**

mastermathsathome.com

How to use this book

Maths — No Problem! created **Master Maths at Home** to help children develop fluency in the subject and a rich understanding of core concepts.

Key features of the Master Maths at Home books include:

- Carefully designed lessons that provide structure, but also allow flexibility in how they're used.

- Speech bubbles containing content designed to spark diverse conversations, with many discussion points that don't have obvious 'right' or 'wrong' answers.

- Rich illustrations that will guide children to a discussion of shapes and units of measurement, allowing them to make connections to the wider world around them.

- Exercises that allow a flexible approach and can be adapted to suit any child's cognitive or functional ability.

- Clearly laid-out pages that encourage children to practise a range of higher-order skills.

- A community of friendly and relatable characters who introduce each lesson and come along as your child progresses through the series.

You can see more guidance on how to use these books at **mastermathsathome.com**.

We're excited to share all the ways you can learn maths!

Maths — No Problem!
mastermathsathome.com
www.mathsnoproblem.com
hello@mathsnoproblem.com

First published in Great Britain in 2022 by
Dorling Kindersley Limited
One Embassy Gardens, 8 Viaduct Gardens, London SW11 7BW
A Penguin Random House Company

The authorised representative in the EEA is Dorling Kindersley
Verlag GmbH. Amulfstr. 124, 80636 Munich, Germany

10 9 8 7 6 5 4 3 2 1
001-327080-Jan/22

A CIP catalogue record for this book is available from the British Library.

ISBN: 978-0-24153-922-4
Printed and bound in the UK

For the curious
www.dk.com

This book was made with Forest Stewardship Council™ certified paper - one small step in DK's commitment to a sustainable future. For more information go to www.dk.com/our-green-pledge

Acknowledgements
The publisher would like to thank the authors and consultants Andy Psarianos, Judy Hornigold, Adam Gifford and Dr Anne Hermanson.

The Castledown typeface has been used with permission from the Colophon Foundry.

Contents

Ruby   Elliott   Amira   Charles   Lulu   Sam   Oak   Holly   Ravi   Emma   Jacob   Hannah

Hundreds

Starter

Charles is helping his dad put sheets of tiles on the bathroom wall. How many tiles are there in total?

Each of these sheets has 100 tiles on it.

Example

We can use these to help us count. Each of these is equal to 100.

There are 10 sheets in total.

We can count in hundreds. 100, 200, 300, 400, ...

...500, 600, 700, 800, 900, 1000 We say **one thousand**.

There are 1000 tiles in total.

	100	one hundred
	200	two hundred
	300	three hundred
	400	four hundred
	500	five hundred
	600	six hundred

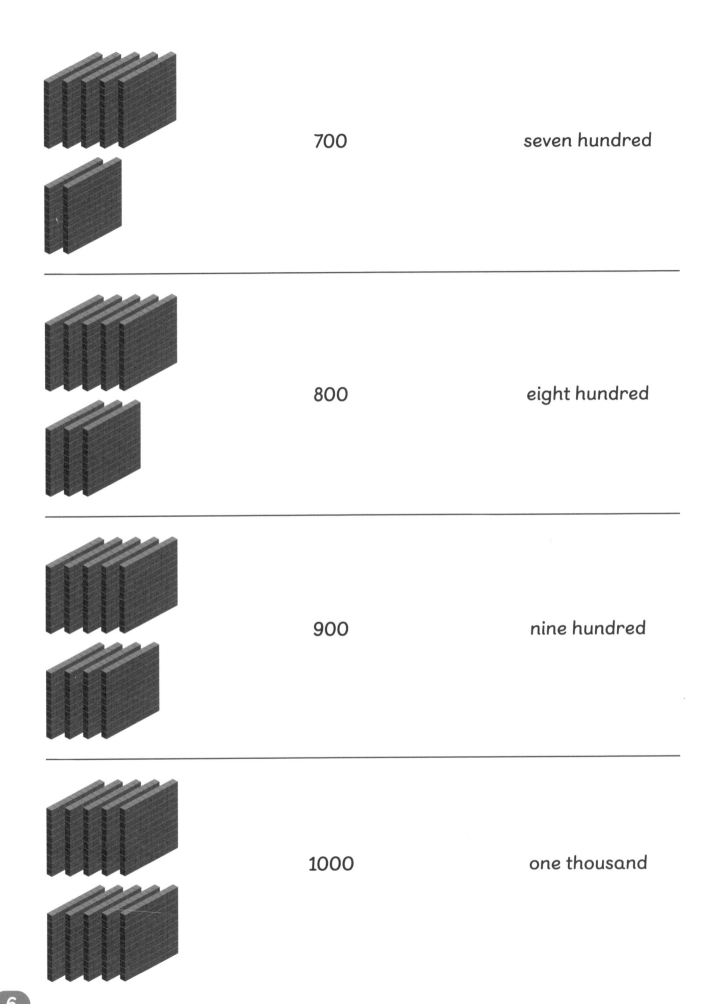

700   seven hundred

800   eight hundred

900   nine hundred

1000   one thousand

Draw lines to match.

500
five hundred

1000
one thousand

700
seven hundred

300
three hundred

Place value

Starter

How many cards does the shopkeeper have altogether?

Example

There are 4 boxes of cards. Each box has 100 cards in it.

There are also 3 packs of 10 cards and 5 loose cards.

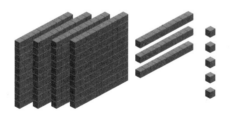

h	t	o
4	3	5

435

400 30 5

435 = 4 hundreds + 3 tens + 5 ones
435 = 400 + 30 + 5

The digit 4 stands for 4 **hundreds** or 400.
The digit 3 stands for 3 **tens** or 30.
The digit 5 stands for 5 **ones** or 5.

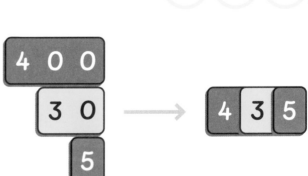

The shopkeeper has 435 cards.
435 is written as **four hundred and thirty-five**.

1 Count in hundreds, tens and ones.
Fill in the blanks.

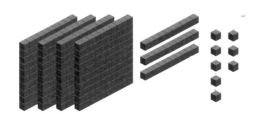

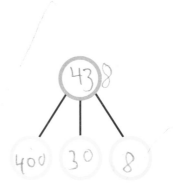

h	t	o
4 0	3⁰	7

400 30 8

438 = 4 hundreds + 30 tens + 8/ ones

438 = 4 + 3 + 8

The value of the digit 4 is 400.

The digit 8 stands for ones.

The digit 30 is in the tens place.

2 Write the words in numerals.

(a) seven hundred and sixty-eight 768

(b) two hundred and ninety-one 291

3 Write the numbers in words.

(a) 593 five hundred and ninety-three

(b) 359 three hundred fifty nine

9

Comparing numbers

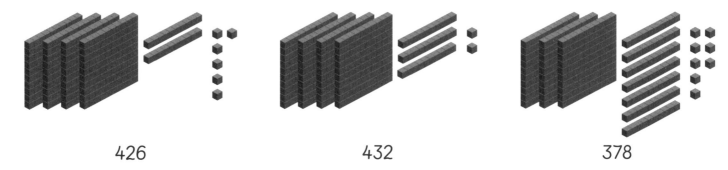

426   432   378

Which number is the greatest and which is the smallest?

Example

h	t	o
4	2	6

h	t	o
4	3	2

h	t	o
3	7	8

First, we should look at the hundreds. 426 and 432 both have 4 hundreds. 378 has 3 hundreds.

378 is the smallest number.

Next, we need to look at the tens. 426 has 2 tens and 432 has 3 tens. 432 has more tens. It is the greatest number.

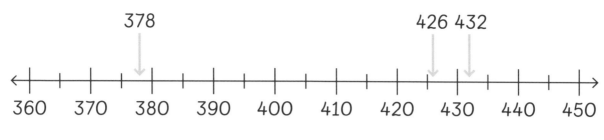

378   426 432

360 370 380 390 400 410 420 430 440 450

We can use a number line to check.

432 is the greatest number and 378 is the smallest number.

Practice

1 Put the numbers in order from greatest to smallest.

(a) 765, 675, 756

765 , 756 , 675

(b) 869, 870, 868

870 , 869 , 868

2 Put the numbers in order from smallest to greatest.

(a) 391, 412, 389

389 , 391 , 412

(b) 897, 789, 879

789 , 879 , 897

3 Use the digits below to make the greatest and the smallest 3-digit numbers.

| 3 | 2 | 7 | 9 | 6 |

976

greatest

236

smallest

Number patterns

How many dots are there?

Example

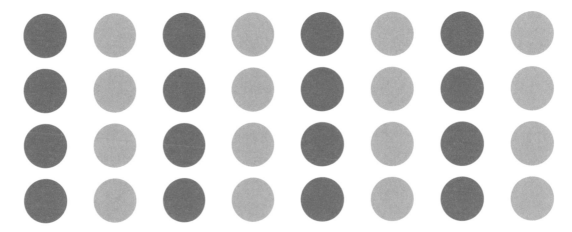

1 There are 8 columns of 4 dots. I can count in fours using a number line.

+4 +4 +4 +4 +4 +4 +4 +4

0 4 8 12 16 20 24 28 32 36 40

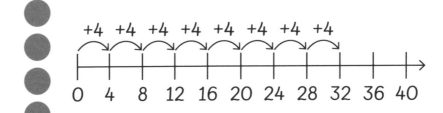

+8   +8   +8   +8

0   8   16   24   32   40

There are 4 rows of 8 dots. I can count in eights using a number line.

2

I have 7 sticker sheets. How many stickers do I have in total?

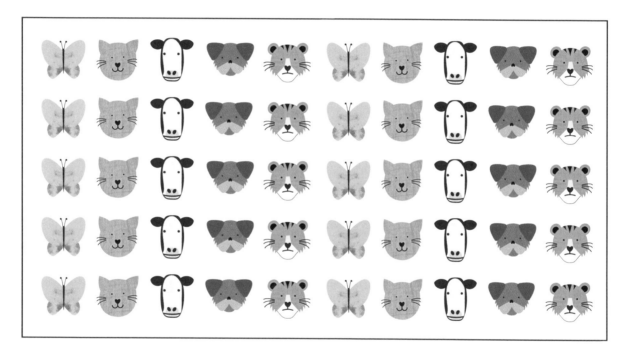

There are 50 stickers on each of Hannah's sheets. She has 7 sheets.

We can count in fifties: 50, 100, 150, 200, 250, 300, 350.

1 Count in fours and shade the numbers in yellow.
Count in eights and shade the numbers in blue.
The first row is done for you.

1	2	3	4	5	6	7	8	9	10
11	12	13	14	15	16	17	18	19	20
21	22	23	24	25	26	27	28	29	30
31	32	33	34	35	36	37	38	39	40
41	42	43	44	45	46	47	48	49	50
51	52	53	54	55	56	57	58	59	60
61	62	63	64	65	66	67	68	69	70
71	72	73	74	75	76	77	78	79	80
81	82	83	84	85	86	87	88	89	90
91	92	93	94	95	96	97	98	99	100

Which numbers are shaded in both yellow and blue?

2 Fill in the blanks.

(a) 8 more than 16 is ☐ .

(b) 4 less than 28 is ☐ .

(c) 50 more than 450 is ☐ .

(d) ☐ more than 68 is 72.

3 Fill in the blanks.

(a) 100 more than 572 is ☐ .

(b) 10 more than 310 is ☐ .

(c) 100 less than 685 is ☐ .

(d) 10 less than 679 is ☐ .

4 Fill in the blanks to complete the number patterns.

(a) 312, 316, ☐ , 324, ☐ , ☐

(b) 200, ☐ , ☐ , 350, ☐ , ☐

(c) 648, 644, ☐ , ☐ , 632, ☐

(d) 728, 720, ☐ , 704, ☐ , 688

Adding without renaming

643 + 4 = ☐

938 + 20 = ☐

565 + 300 = ☐

In what ways can these numbers be added?

Example

For 643 + 4 we only need to add the ones.

643 + 4

640   3

643 + 4 = 647

4 + 3 = 7

640 + 7 = 647

h	t	o
6	4	3
+		4
6	4	7

I can use a similar method for 938 + 20. We only need to add the tens.

938 + 20

908   30

938 + 20 = 958

30 + 20 = 50

908 + 50 = 958

h	t	o
9	3	8
+	2	0
9	5	8

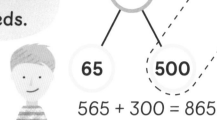

For 565 + 300 we only need to add the hundreds.

565 + 300

65   500

500 + 300 = 800
65 + 800 = 865

565 + 300 = 865

	h	t	o
	5	6	5
+	3	0	0
	8	6	5

Practice

1 Complete the number bonds and add.

(a)
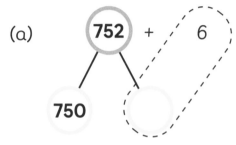

752 + 6

750

752 + 6 = ☐

(b)

843 + 50

803

843 + 50 = ☐

(c)

634 + 300

634 + 300 = ☐

2 Add and fill in the blanks.

(a) 314 + 5 = ☐

(b) 453 + 500 = ☐

(c) 221 + 50 = ☐

Adding with renaming (part 1)

Starter

Elliott read 237 pages of his novel last week and 218 pages this week. How many pages has Elliott read in total?

Example

We need to add 237 and 218.

Step 1   Add the ones.
          Rename the ones.

7 ones + 8 ones = 15 ones
15 ones = 1 ten and 5 ones

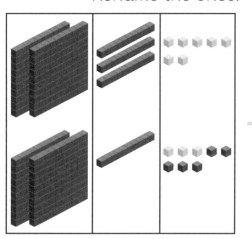

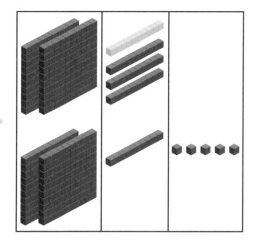

```
    h   t   o
            1
    2   3   7
+   2   1   8
_____
            5
```

Step 2　Add the tens.　　1 ten + 3 tens + 1 ten = 5 tens

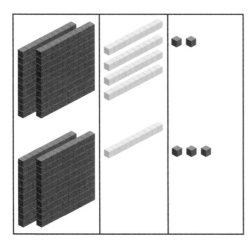

h	t	o
	^{1}	
2	3	7
+ 2	1	8
	5	5

Step 3　Add the hundreds.　　2 hundreds + 2 hundreds = 4 hundreds

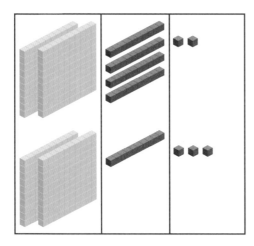
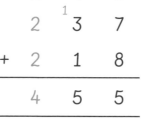

h	t	o
	^{1}	
2	3	7
+ 2	1	8
4	5	5

237 + 218 = 455

Elliott has read 455 pages in total.

Practice

Add.

1　426 and 349

h	t	o
4	2	6
+ 3	4	9

2　208 and 463

h	t	o
2	0	8
+ 4	6	3

3　569 and 319

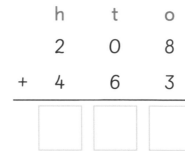

h	t	o
5	6	9
+ 3	1	9

Adding with renaming (part 2)

Starter

There are 382 people waiting in the queue for the amusement park to open. A bus drops off another 35 people who also join the queue.

How many people are now in the queue for the amusement park?

Example

We need to add 382 and 35.

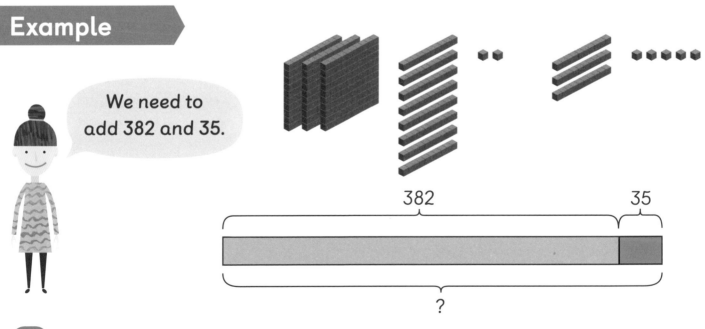

382   35

?

Add 382 and 35.

Step 1   Add the ones.

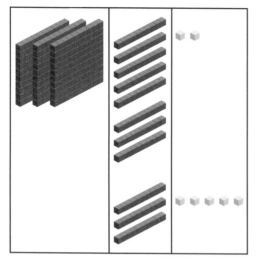

h	t	o
3	8	2
+	3	5
		7

Step 2   Add the tens.
8 tens + 3 tens = 11 tens
Rename the tens.
11 tens = 1 hundred + 1 ten

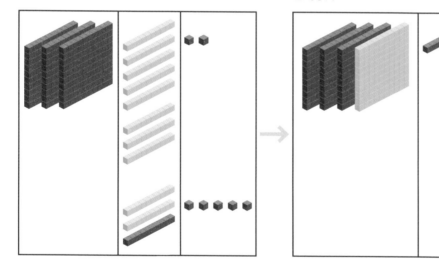

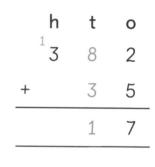

h	t	o
^{1}3	8	2
+	3	5
	1	7

Step 3   Add the hundreds.
1 hundred + 3 hundreds = 4 hundreds

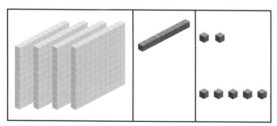

h	t	o
^{1}3	8	2
+	3	5
4	1	7

382 + 35 = 417
There are now 417 people in the queue for the amusement park.

1 Add.

(a)
h	t	o
4	5	6
+	2	2

☐ ☐ ☐

(b)
h	t	o
5	5	2
+	8	6

☐ ☐ ☐

(c)
h	t	o
	8	0
+ 7	2	0

☐ ☐ ☐

(d)
h	t	o
2	6	5
+	4	3

☐ ☐ ☐

2 Complete the equations by filling in the blanks.

(a) $281 + 41 = $ ☐

(b) $74 + 635 = $ ☐

(c) $125 + 92 = $ ☐

(d) $470 + 50 = $ ☐

(e) $64 + 275 = $ ☐

(f) $795 + 93 = $ ☐

(g) ☐ $+ 20 = 600$

(h) $99 + $ ☐ $= 738$

3 There are 251 children already sitting down for the school assembly.
58 Year 6 children then arrive and take their seats.
How many children are now sitting down?

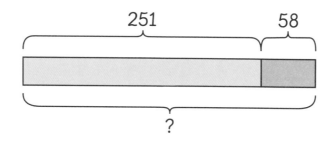

children are now sitting down.

Elliott and Oak like to make necklaces with beads.
Elliott has 134 more beads than Oak. Oak has 80 beads.
How many beads does Elliott have?

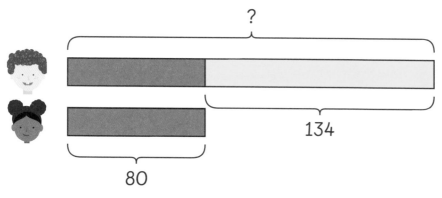

Elliott has ⬜ beads.

Adding with renaming (part 3)

Starter

417 people bought tickets for the amusement park in the first hour. During the next hour, 294 people bought tickets for the amusement park.

How many tickets did the amusement park sell in the first 2 hours?

Example

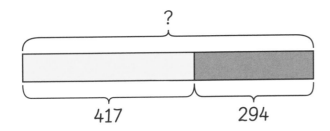

We need to add the two numbers to find the total.

Add 417 and 294.

Step 1   Add the ones.   7 ones + 4 ones = 11 ones
            Rename the ones.   11 ones = 1 ten + 1 one

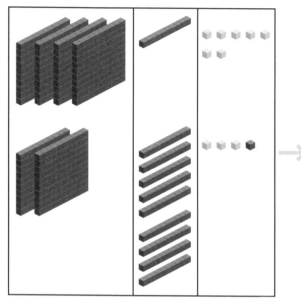 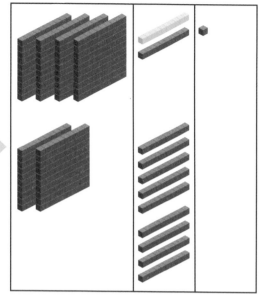

	h	t	o
	4	¹1	7
+	2	9	4
			1

Step 2   Add the tens.   1 ten + 10 tens = 11 tens
            Rename the tens.   11 tens = 1 hundred + 1 ten

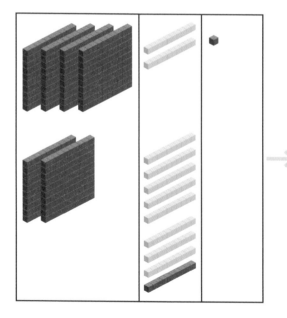 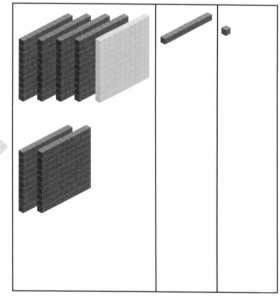

	h	t	o
	¹4	¹1	7
+	2	9	4
		1	1

Step 3 Add the hundreds.

1 hundred + 4 hundreds + 2 hundreds = 7 hundreds

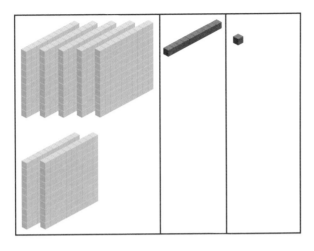

$$\begin{array}{ccc} h & t & o \\ {}^1 4 & {}^1 1 & 7 \\ + \quad 2 & 9 & 4 \\ \hline 7 & 1 & 1 \end{array}$$

417 + 294 = 711

The amusement park sold 711 tickets in the first 2 hours.

Practice

1 Add.

(a)

h	t	o
2	6	5
+ 3	7	8

(b)

h	t	o
4	7	2
+ 1	9	9

(c)

h	t	o
2	7	8
+ 2	2	2

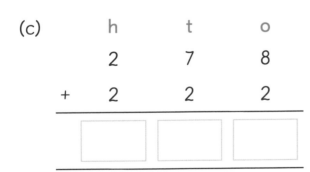

(d)

h	t	o
3	3	6
+ 1	6	4

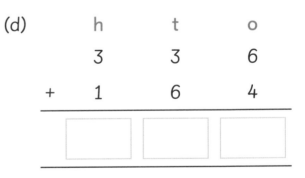

(e)

h	t	o
6	9	9
+ 1	8	9

(f)

h	t	o
2	8	9
+ 5	9	9

2 A farmer is growing pumpkins for Halloween.
She has 376 pumpkins growing on one patch of land.
She has 227 pumpkins growing on another patch.
How many pumpkins does the farmer have on her
2 patches of land?

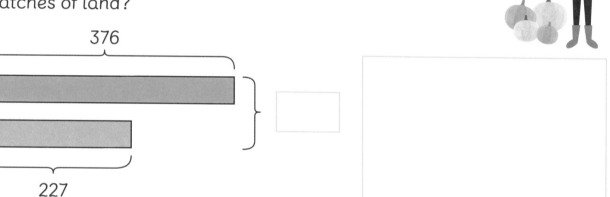

376

227

The farmer has ☐ pumpkins growing on her 2 patches of land.

3 One football player scored 177 league
goals in his career. Another football player
scored 187 league goals in his career.
How many goals did the two players score
in their careers altogether?

The two players scored ☐ goals in their careers altogether.

Subtracting without renaming

$$796 - 4 =$$
$$467 - 50 =$$
$$978 - 200 =$$

In what ways can these numbers be subtracted?

Example

For 796 – 4 you only need to subtract the ones.

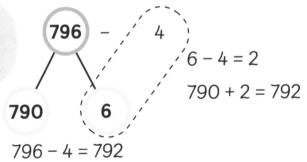

796 – 4

790   6

796 – 4 = 792

$6 - 4 = 2$

$790 + 2 = 792$

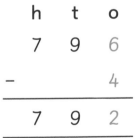

h	t	o
7	9	6
–		4
7	9	2

For 467 – 50 we can subtract just the tens.

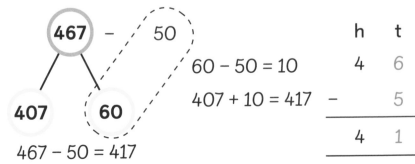

467 – 50

407   60

467 – 50 = 417

$60 - 50 = 10$

$407 + 10 = 417$

h	t	o
4	6	7
–	5	0
4	1	7

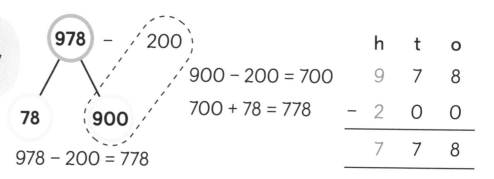

For 978 – 200 we can subtract only the hundreds.

$978 - 200$

$900 - 200 = 700$
$700 + 78 = 778$

$978 - 200 = 778$

h	t	o
9	7	8
– 2	0	0
7	7	8

Practice

1 Complete the number bonds and subtract.

(a) $576 - 5$ 570

$576 - 5 = \boxed{}$

(b) $284 - 30$ 204

$284 - 30 = \boxed{}$

(c) $419 - 200$

$419 - 200 = \boxed{}$

2 Subtract and fill in the blanks.

(a) $297 - 6 = \boxed{}$

(b) $483 - 50 = \boxed{}$

(c) $949 - 700 = \boxed{}$

Subtracting with renaming (part 1)

Starter

What does Oak need to do to find the answer?

Example

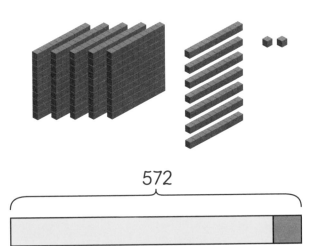

Oak needs to subtract to find the answer but there are not enough ones in 572.

We can rename 1 ten to 10 ones. We will then have 12 ones in total to subtract from.

Subtract 56 from 572.

Step 1   Rename 1 ten into 10 ones.
          Subtract the ones.
          12 ones – 6 ones = 6 ones

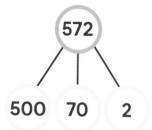

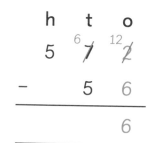

$$
\begin{array}{r}
\text{h} \quad \text{t} \quad \text{o} \\
5 \quad \overset{6}{\cancel{7}} \quad \overset{12}{\cancel{2}} \\
- \quad 5 \quad 6 \\
\hline
 \quad 6 \\
\hline
\end{array}
$$

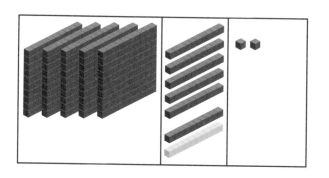

Step 2   Subtract the tens.
          6 tens – 5 tens = 1 ten

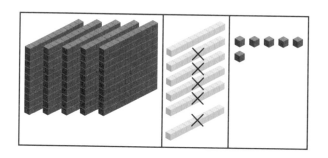

$$
\begin{array}{r}
\text{h} \quad \text{t} \quad \text{o} \\
5 \quad \overset{6}{\cancel{7}} \quad \overset{12}{\cancel{2}} \\
- \quad 5 \quad 6 \\
\hline
 \quad 1 \quad 6 \\
\hline
\end{array}
$$

Step 3   Subtract the hundreds.
          5 hundreds – 0 hundreds = 5 hundreds

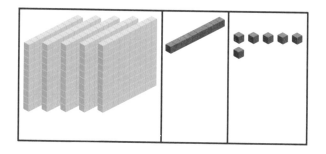

$$
\begin{array}{r}
\text{h} \quad \text{t} \quad \text{o} \\
5 \quad \overset{6}{\cancel{7}} \quad \overset{12}{\cancel{2}} \\
- \quad 5 \quad 6 \\
\hline
5 \quad 1 \quad 6 \\
\hline
\end{array}
$$

572 – 56 = 516

1 Subtract.

(a)

h	t	o
2	7	6
−	5	9

(b)

h	t	o
7	9	3
−	2	7

(c)

h	t	o
5	3	6
− 1	2	8

(d)

h	t	o
9	5	4
− 5	4	6

(e)

h	t	o
8	7	6
− 3	0	9

(f)

h	t	o
6	9	5
− 1	2	8

2 Holly's high score in a video game is 160 points more than Ravi's high score. Holly's high score is 930 points.

(a) What is Ravi's high score in the video game?

Ravi's high score in the video game is [   ].

(b) Charles's high score is 680 points.
What is the difference between Charles's high score
and Holly's high score?

The difference between Charles's high score and

Holly's high score is [   ] .

(c) Who has more points, Ravi or Charles?

[   ] has more points.

(d) How many more points does he have?

He has [   ] more points.

Subtracting with renaming (part 2)

Starter

There are 506 students at Evergreen Primary School.
142 of the children wear glasses.

How many of the children do not wear glasses?

Example

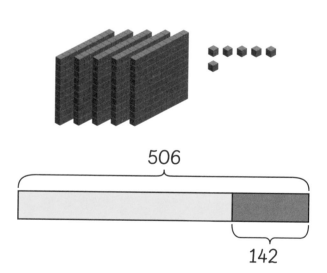

506

142

We need to subtract 142 from 506 but there are not enough tens.

We can rename 1 hundred into 10 tens.

Subtract 142 from 506.

Step 1   Subtract the ones.
          6 ones − 2 ones = 4 ones

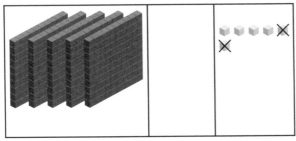

```
  h   t   o
  5   0   6
−  1   4   2
_____
          4
```

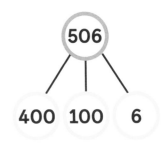

Step 2   Rename 1 hundred into 10 tens.
          Subtract the tens.
          10 tens − 4 tens = 6 tens

```
      h       t   o
     4 5   10 0   6
  −    1      4   2
  _____
              6   4
```

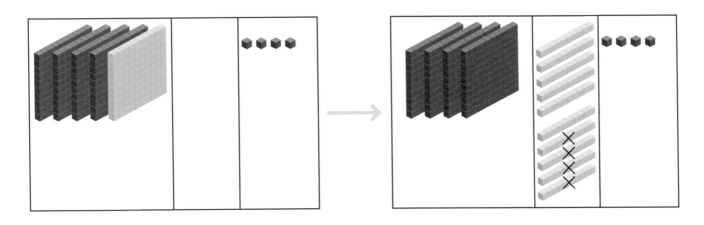

Step 3   Subtract the hundreds.
          4 hundreds − 1 hundred = 3 hundreds

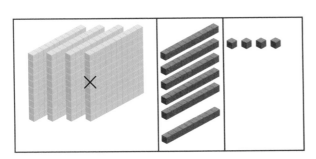

```
      h       t   o
     4 5   10 0   6
  −    1      4   2
  _____
      3       6   4
```

506 − 142 = 364
364 children do not wear glasses.

1 Subtract.

(a)

h	t	o
2	5	8
−	6	3

(b)

h	t	o
7	1	9
−	4	5

(c)

h	t	o
9	1	5
− 7	5	3

(d)

h	t	o
9	1	5
− 1	6	2

(e)

h	t	o
4	4	4
− 1	7	3

(f)

h	t	o
5	5	5
− 2	8	4

2 A car park has 413 parking spots.
191 of the parking spots have cars
in them.
How many parking spots are empty?

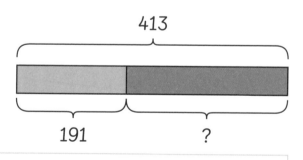

413

191   ?

There are [ ] empty parking spots in the car park.

3 (a) A snack bar sold 318 burgers in one week.
The week after, it sold 151 burgers.
How many more burgers did it sell in the first week than in the second week?

318

151

?

The snack bar sold [ ] more burgers in the first week than in the second week.

(b) There is a cafe on the same road as the snack bar.
The cafe sold 202 burgers in the first week.
How many more burgers did the snack bar sell than the cafe in the first week?

The snack bar sold [ ] more burgers than the cafe in the first week.

Subtracting with renaming (part 3)

Starter

In the late evening, 830 black crows settle down in the woods to roost for the night. In the early morning, 367 crows fly away.

When crows or other birds settle for the night we call it roosting.

How many crows are still roosting in the woods?

Example

We need to subtract 367 from 830.

There are not enough ones or tens to subtract with.

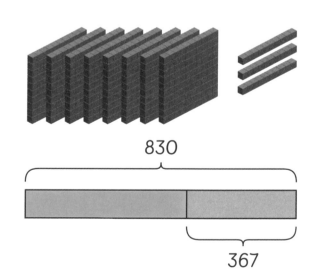

830

367

38

We can take 1 hundred from the 8 hundreds and rename it. We will then have enough ones and tens to subtract 367.

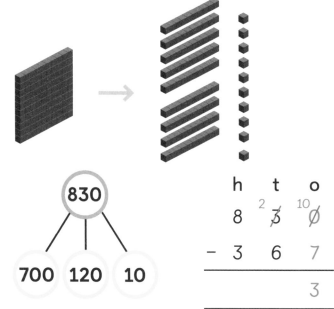

Subtract 367 from 830.

Step 1   Rename 1 ten into 10 ones.

10 ones − 7 ones = 3 ones

830 → 700   120   10

	h	t	o
	8	²3̶	¹⁰0̶
−	3	6	7
			3

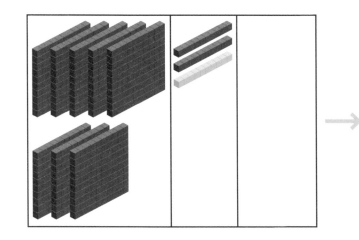

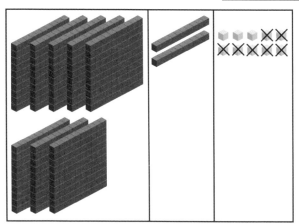

Step 2   Rename 1 hundred into 10 tens.
Subtract the tens.

12 tens − 6 tens = 6 tens

	h	t	o
	⁷8̶	¹²3̶	¹⁰0̶
−	3	6	7
		6	3

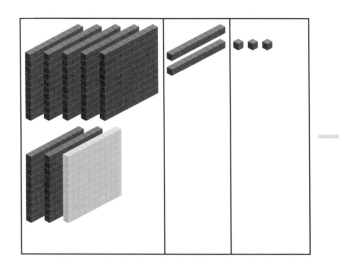

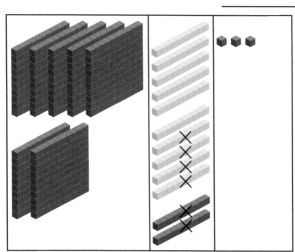

Step 3   Subtract the hundreds.

7 hundreds − 3 hundreds = 4 hundreds

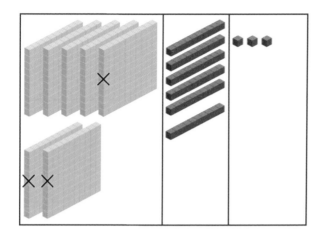

830 − 367 = 463

There are 463 crows still roosting in the woods.

Practice

1   Subtract.

(a)

h	t	o
7	0	6
−	3	8

(b)

h	t	o
8	0	2
−	2	7

(c)

h	t	o
4	0	3
− 3	4	5

(d)

h	t	o
2	0	4
− 1	1	6

(e)

h	t	o
3	0	3
− 2	0	4

(f)

h	t	o
7	0	5
− 6	0	6

(g)

h	t	o
8	0	7
− 5	4	9

(h)

h	t	o
8	0	1
− 5	4	9

2 Emma scored 206 points in her video game on Tuesday.
On Wednesday, she scored 28 points less than she scored on Tuesday.
How many points did Emma score on Wednesday?

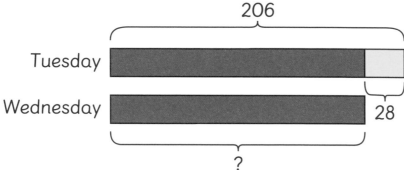

206

Tuesday

Wednesday   28

?

Emma scored [ ] points on Wednesday.

Review and challenge

1 Count in hundreds, tens and ones.

Fill in the blanks.

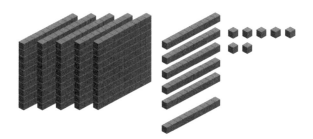 

h	t	o

$\boxed{}$ = $\boxed{}$ hundreds + $\boxed{}$ tens + $\boxed{}$ ones

$\boxed{}$ = $\boxed{}$ + $\boxed{}$ + $\boxed{}$

The value of the digit 5 is $\boxed{}$.

The digit 7 stands for $\boxed{}$.

The digit $\boxed{}$ is in the tens place.

2 (a) Write the words in numerals.

eight hundred and sixty-four $\boxed{}$

(b) Write the number in words.

723 $\boxed{}$

3 Put the numbers in order from greatest to smallest.

(a) 579, 521, 920

[ ] , [ ] , [ ]

(b) 559, 641, 425

[ ] , [ ] , [ ]

4 Put the numbers in order from smallest to greatest.

(a) 373, 725, 223

[ ] , [ ] , [ ]

(b) 747, 338, 350

[ ] , [ ] , [ ]

5 Fill in the blanks.

(a) 8 more than 32 is [ ] .

(b) 4 less than 36 is [ ] .

(c) 50 more than 300 is [ ] .

(d) [ ] more than 28 is 32.

(e) 10 more than 310 is [ ] .

(f) 100 more than 628 is [ ] .

(g) 100 less than 515 is [ ] .

(h) 10 less than 867 is [ ] .

6 Fill in the blanks to complete the number patterns.

(a) 592, 596, [ ] , 604

(b) 400, [ ] , [ ] , 550

(c) 648, 644, [ ] , [ ]

(d) 672, 664, [ ] , 648

7 Add.

(a)

	h	t	o
	6	5	3
+	1	2	8

(b)

	h	t	o
	2	9	0
+	6	2	7

(c)

	h	t	o
	2	6	7
+	6	3	6

(d)

	h	t	o
	4	5	5
+	2	5	7

8 Subtract.

(a)

	h	t	o
	9	3	5
–	7	2	3

(b)

	h	t	o
	2	8	6
–	1	6	7

(c)

	h	t	o
	8	5	3
–	5	7	2

(d)

	h	t	o
	7	0	0
–	3	8	2

9 Solve and fill in the blanks.

Emma and Jacob both sold raffle tickets at the school fete. Jacob sold 376 raffle tickets. He sold 187 fewer raffle tickets than Emma sold.

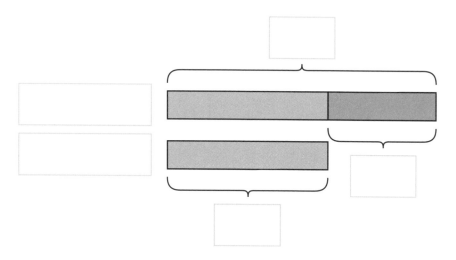

How many raffle tickets did Emma sell?

Emma sold ☐ raffle tickets.

How many raffle tickets did the children sell altogether?

Altogether, the children sold ☐ raffle tickets.

Answers

Page 7

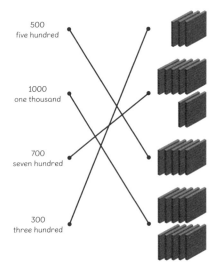

Page 9

h	t	o
4	3	8

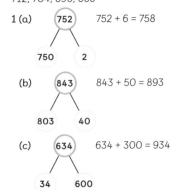

438 = 4 hundreds + 3 tens + 8 ones; 438 = 400 + 30 + 8. The value of the digit 4 is 400. The digit 8 stands for 8 ones. The digit 3 is in the tens place. **2 (a)** 768 **(b)** 291 **3 (a)** five hundred and ninety-three **(b)** three hundred and fifty-nine

Page 11

1 (a) 765, 756, 675 **(b)** 870, 869, 868 **2 (a)** 389, 391, 412 **(b)** 789, 879, 897 **3** greatest: 976; smallest: 236

Page 14

1

1	2	3	4	5	6	7	8	9	10
11	12	13	14	15	16	17	18	19	20
21	22	23	24	25	26	27	28	29	30
31	32	33	34	35	36	37	38	39	40
41	42	43	44	45	46	47	48	49	50
51	52	53	54	55	56	57	58	59	60
61	62	63	64	65	66	67	68	69	70
71	72	73	74	75	76	77	78	79	80
81	82	83	84	85	86	87	88	89	90
91	92	93	94	95	96	97	98	99	100

8, 16, 24, 32, 40, 48, 56, 64, 72, 80, 88, 96

Page 15

2 (a) 8 more than 16 is 24. **(b)** 4 less than 28 is 24. **(c)** 50 more than 450 is 500. **(d)** 4 more than 68 is 72. **3 (a)** 100 more than 572 is 672. **(b)** 10 more than 310 is 320. **(c)** 100 less than 685 is 585. **(d)** 10 less than 679 is 669. **4 (a)** 312, 316, 320, 324, 328, 332 **(b)** 200, 250, 300, 350, 400, 450 **(c)** 648, 644, 640, 636, 632, 628 **(d)** 728, 720, 712, 704, 696, 688

Page 17

1 (a) 752 → 750, 2   752 + 6 = 758

(b) 843 → 803, 40   843 + 50 = 893

(c) 634 → 34, 600   634 + 300 = 934

2 (a) 314 + 5 = 319 **(b)** 453 + 500 = 953 **(c)** 221 + 50 = 271

Page 19

1
h	t	o
4	¹2	6
+ 3	4	9
7	7	5

2
h	t	o
2	¹0	8
+ 4	6	3
6	7	1

3
h	t	o
5	¹6	9
+ 3	1	9
8	8	8

Page 22

1 (a)
h	t	o
4	5	6
+	2	2
4	7	8

(b)
h	t	o
¹5	5	2
+	8	6
6	3	8

(c)
h	t	o
¹	8	0
+ 7	2	0
8	0	0

(d)
h	t	o
¹2	6	5
+	4	3
3	0	8

2 (a) 281 + 41 = 322 **(b)** 74 + 635 = 709 **(c)** 125 + 92 = 217 **(d)** 470 + 50 = 520 **(e)** 64 + 275 = 339 **(f)** 795 + 93 = 888 **(g)** 580 + 20 = 600 **(h)** 99 + 639 = 738

Page 23

3 309 children are now sitting down. **4** Elliott has 214 beads.

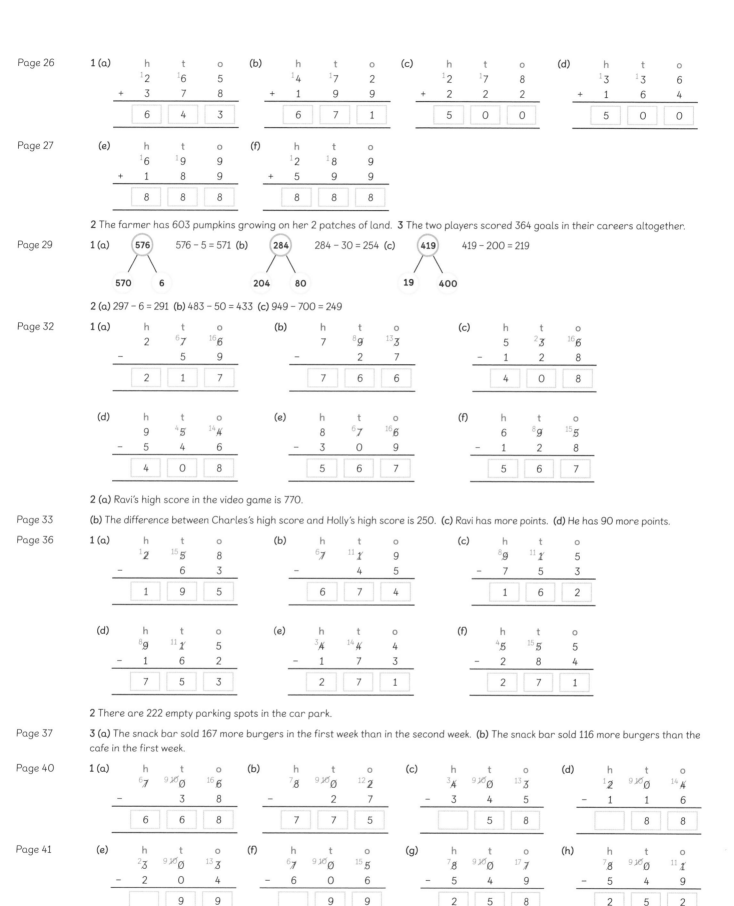

Page 26　　1 (a)

h	t	o
¹2	¹6	5
+ 3	7	8
6	**4**	**3**

(b)

h	t	o
¹4	¹7	2
+ 1	9	9
6	**7**	**1**

(c)

h	t	o
¹2	¹7	8
+ 2	2	2
5	**0**	**0**

(d)

h	t	o
¹3	¹3	6
+ 1	6	4
5	**0**	**0**

Page 27　　(e)

h	t	o
¹6	¹9	9
+ 1	8	9
8	**8**	**8**

(f)

h	t	o
¹2	¹8	9
+ 5	9	9
8	**8**	**8**

2 The farmer has 603 pumpkins growing on her 2 patches of land.　**3** The two players scored 364 goals in their careers altogether.

Page 29　　1 (a) ⟨576⟩　576 – 5 = 571　(b) ⟨284⟩　284 – 30 = 254　(c) ⟨419⟩　419 – 200 = 219

570　6　　204　80　　19　400

2 (a) 297 – 6 = 291　(b) 483 – 50 = 433　(c) 949 – 700 = 249

Page 32　　1 (a)

h	t	o
2	⁶7̶	¹⁶6̶
–	5	9
2	**1**	**7**

(b)

h	t	o
7	⁸9̶	¹³3̶
–	2	7
7	**6**	**6**

(c)

h	t	o
5	²3̶	¹⁶6̶
– 1	2	8
4	**0**	**8**

(d)

h	t	o
9	⁴5̶	¹⁴4̶
– 5	4	6
4	**0**	**8**

(e)

h	t	o
8	⁶7̶	¹⁶6̶
– 3	0	9
5	**6**	**7**

(f)

h	t	o
6	⁸9̶	¹⁵5̶
– 1	2	8
5	**6**	**7**

2 (a) Ravi's high score in the video game is 770.

Page 33　　(b) The difference between Charles's high score and Holly's high score is 250.　(c) Ravi has more points.　(d) He has 90 more points.

Page 36　　1 (a)

h	t	o
¹2̶	¹⁵5̶	8
–	6	3
1	**9**	**5**

(b)

h	t	o
⁶7̶	¹¹1̶	9
–	4	5
6	**7**	**4**

(c)

h	t	o
⁸9̶	¹¹1̶	5
– 7	5	3
1	**6**	**2**

(d)

h	t	o
⁸9̶	¹¹1̶	5
– 1	6	2
7	**5**	**3**

(e)

h	t	o
³4̶	¹⁴4̶	4
– 1	7	3
2	**7**	**1**

(f)

h	t	o
⁴5̶	¹⁵5̶	5
– 2	8	4
2	**7**	**1**

2 There are 222 empty parking spots in the car park.

Page 37　　3 (a) The snack bar sold 167 more burgers in the first week than in the second week.　(b) The snack bar sold 116 more burgers than the cafe in the first week.

Page 40　　1 (a)

h	t	o
⁶7̶	⁹¹⁰0̶	¹⁶6̶
–	3	8
6	**6**	**8**

(b)

h	t	o
⁷8̶	⁹¹⁰0̶	¹²2̶
–	2	7
7	**7**	**5**

(c)

h	t	o
³4̶	⁹¹⁰0̶	¹³3̶
– 3	4	5
	5	**8**

(d)

h	t	o
¹2̶	⁹¹⁰0̶	¹⁴4̶
– 1	1	6
	8	**8**

Page 41　　(e)

h	t	o
²3̶	⁹¹⁰0̶	¹³3̶
– 2	0	4
	9	**9**

(f)

h	t	o
⁶7̶	⁹¹⁰0̶	¹⁵5̶
– 6	0	6
	9	**9**

(g)

h	t	o
⁷8̶	⁹¹⁰0̶	¹⁷7̶
– 5	4	9
2	**5**	**8**

(h)

h	t	o
⁷8̶	⁹¹⁰0̶	¹¹1̶
– 5	4	9
2	**5**	**2**

2 Emma scored 178 points on Wednesday.

Answers continued

Page 42

1

h	t	o
5	6	7

567 = 5 hundreds + 6 tens + 7 ones;   567 = 500 + 60 + 7. The value of the digit 5 is 500. The digit 7 stands for 7 ones. The digit 6 is in the tens place.

2 (a) 864 **(b)** seven hundred and twenty-three

Page 43

3 (a) 920, 579, 521 **(b)** 641, 559, 425 **4 (a)** 223, 373, 725 **(b)** 338, 350, 747 **5 (a)** 8 more than 32 is 40. **(b)** 4 less than 36 is 32. **(c)** 50 more than 300 is 350. **(d)** 4 more than 28 is 32. **(e)** 10 more than 310 is 320. **(f)** 100 more than 628 is 728. **(g)** 100 less than 515 is 415. **(h)** 10 less than 867 is 857. **6 (a)** 592, 596, 600, 604 **(b)** 400, 450, 500, 550 **(c)** 648, 644, 640, 636 **(d)** 672, 664, 656, 648

Page 44

7 (a)

h	t	o
6	¹5	3
+ 1	2	8
7	8	1

(b)

h	t	o
¹2	9	0
+ 6	2	7
9	1	7

(c)

h	t	o
¹2	¹6	7
+ 6	3	6
9	0	3

(d)

h	t	o
¹4	¹5	5
+ 2	5	7
7	1	2

8 (a)

h	t	o
9	3	5
− 7	2	3
2	1	2

(b)

h	t	o
2	⁷8	¹⁶6
− 1	6	7
1	1	9

(c)

h	t	o
⁷8	¹⁵5	3
− 5	7	2
2	8	1

(d)

h	t	o
⁶7	⁹¹0	¹⁰0
− 3	8	2
3	1	8

Page 45

9

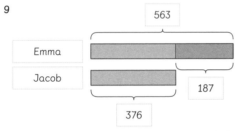

Emma	
Jacob	

563

187

376

Emma sold 563 raffle tickets. Altogether, the children sold 939 raffle tickets.

hundred